Tropical Flowers Lace Curtain Filet Crochet Pattern

Tropical Flowers
Lace Curtain
Filet Crochet Pattern

Complete Instructions and Chart

designed by Mary E. Fitch

edited by Claudia Botterweg

EIGHTTHREEPRESS
Phoenix, Arizona, USA

Original pattern design by Mary E. Fitch, first published in 1920
Pattern rewritten, expanded, edited and charted by Claudia Botterweg,
published in 2015 by Eight Three Press
ISBN-13: 978-1511546225
ISBN-10: 1511546220
Every effort has been made to ensure that all the infor-
mation in this book is accurate. If you have questions or
comments about this pattern, please contact Claudia Botterweg at
http://claudiabotterweg.com/contact

Contents

Introduction

Bring a touch of the tropics to your home decor with palm trees, flowering vines, and a basket full of tropical flowers. Originally designed in 1920 by Mary E. Fitch, the pattern is ideal to use for a valance by sewing plastic rings to the top.

Size & Yardage

The approximate size of the finished piece will change when made with different sizes of thread and hooks. Approximate yardage needed for each thread size varies also.

For best results, make a gauge swatch before you begin.

Size 5 thread (about 3.6 squares/inch)
Width: 28 ¼", Height: 21"
Amount of thread required: 1,300 yards + 100 for tassels
Suggested hook: Size 3 steel

Size 10 thread (about 4.3 squares/inch)
Width: 23 ¼", Height: 16 ½"
Amount of thread required: 850 yards + 100 for tassels
Suggested hook: Size 7 steel

Size 20 thread (about 4.5 squares/inch)
Width: 22 ¼", Height: 15 ¾"
Amount of thread required: 810 yards + 100 for tassels
Suggested hook: Size 10 steel

Size 30 thread (about 4.7 squares/inch)
Width: 21 ¼", Height: 15"
Amount of thread required: 760 yards + 100 for tassels
Suggested hook: Size 11 steel

Size 50 thread (about 6 squares/inch)
  Width: 16", Height: 11 ¾"
  Amount of thread required: 480 yards + 100 for tassels
  Suggested hook: Size 12 steel

Size 80 thread (about 7 squares/inch)
  Width: 14", Height: 10 ½"
  Amount of thread required: 375 yards + 100 for tassels
  Suggested hook: Size 14 steel

Tropical Flowers Written Instructions

Abbreviations used in this pattern
( ) work instructions within parentheses as many times as directed
* * work instructions within asterisks as many times as directed
ch: chain stitch
dc: double crochet
sk: skip the indicated amount of stitches
sl st: slip stitch
dtr: double treble crochet
space: ch 2, sk 2, dc in next st. At the beginning of a row, ch 5 for the first space.
block: dc in next 3 stitches.

Decreases for a single space are made in the previous row by: sk 2, dtr in next stitch. This makes it unnecessary to slip stitch across squares at the beginning of the decrease row.

Chain 338, turn.
Row 1: Dc in 8th ch from hook, 110 spaces, turn. 111 squares.
Row 2: 111 spaces, turn.
Row 3: (2 spaces, 1 block) twice, (2 spaces, 4 blocks, 2 spaces, 1 block) 5 times, 2 spaces, 5 blocks, 2 spaces, (1 block, 2 spaces, 4 blocks, 2 spaces) 5 times, (1 block, 2 spaces) twice, turn.
Row 4: 3 spaces, 11 blocks, (1 space, 8 blocks) 4 times, 1 space, 9 blocks, 1 space, (8 blocks, 1 space) 4 times, 11 blocks, 3 spaces, turn.
Row 5: 3 spaces, 1 block, 1 space, 1 block, 2 spaces, (4 blocks, 2 spaces, 1 block, 2 spaces) 5 times, 5 blocks, (2 spaces, 1 block, 2 spaces, 4 blocks) 5 times, 2 spaces, 1 block, 1 space, 1 block, 3 spaces, turn.

Row 6: 2 spaces, 5 blocks, 48 spaces, 1 block, 48 spaces, 5 blocks, 2 spaces, turn.

Row 7: 3 spaces, 1 block, 1 space, 3 blocks, 47 spaces, 1 block, 47 spaces, 3 blocks, 1 space, 1 block, 3 spaces, turn.

Row 8: 3 spaces, 1 block, 2 spaces, 2 blocks, 24 spaces, 2 blocks, 20 spaces, 1 block, 1 space, 1 block, 20 spaces, 2 blocks, 24 spaces, 2 blocks, 2 spaces, 1 block, 3 spaces, turn.

Row 9: 2 spaces, 3 blocks, 3 spaces, 1 block, 23 spaces, 2 blocks, 20 spaces, 1 block, 1 space, 1 block, 20 spaces, 2 blocks, 23 spaces, 1 block, 3 spaces, 3 blocks, 2 spaces, turn.

Row 10: 2 spaces, 3 blocks, 11 spaces, 3 blocks, 12 spaces, 4 blocks, 19 spaces, 1 block, 1 space, 1 block, 19 spaces, 4 blocks, 12 spaces, 3 blocks, 11 spaces, 3 blocks, 2 spaces, turn.

Row 11: 2 spaces, 3 blocks, 10 spaces, 4 blocks, 6 spaces, 3 blocks, 3 spaces, 4 blocks, 3 spaces, 3 blocks, 13 spaces, 1 block, 1 space, 1 block, 13 spaces, 3 blocks, 3 spaces, 4 blocks, 3 spaces, 3 blocks, 6 spaces, 4 blocks, 10 spaces, 3 blocks, 2 spaces, turn.

Row 12: 2 spaces, 3 blocks, 9 spaces, 5 blocks, 6 spaces, 4 blocks, (2 spaces, 4 blocks) twice, 13 spaces, 1 block, 1 space, 1 block, 13 spaces, (4 blocks, 2 spaces) twice, 4 blocks, 6 spaces, 5 blocks, 9 spaces, 3 blocks, 2 spaces, turn.

Row 13: 3 spaces, 1 block, 9 spaces, 5 blocks, 7 spaces, 4 blocks, (2 spaces, 4 blocks) twice, 14 spaces, 1 block, 14 spaces, (4 blocks, 2 spaces) twice, 4 blocks, 7 spaces, 5 blocks, 9 spaces, 1 block, 3 spaces, turn.

Row 14: 3 spaces, 1 block, 8 spaces, 5 blocks, 9 spaces, 4 blocks, (1 space, 4 blocks) twice, 10 spaces, 3 blocks, 2 spaces, 1 block, 2 spaces, 3 blocks, 10 spaces, (4 blocks, 1 space) twice, 4 blocks, 9 spaces, 5 blocks, 8 spaces, 1 block, 3 spaces, turn.

Row 15: 2 spaces, 1 block, 1 space, 1 block, 7 spaces, 5 blocks, 10 spaces, 3 blocks, 1 space, 4 blocks, 1 space, 3 blocks, 10 spaces, 1 block, 3 spaces, 2 blocks, 1 space, 2 blocks, 3 spaces, 1 block, 10 spaces, 3 blocks, 1 space, 4 blocks, 1 space, 3 blocks, 10 spaces, 5 blocks, 7 spaces, 1 block, 1 space, 1 block, 2 spaces, turn.

Row 16: 3 spaces, 1 block, 8 spaces, 4 blocks, 14 spaces, 1 block, 1 space, 2 blocks, 1 space, 1 block, 13 spaces, 1 block, 5 spaces, 1 block, 5 spaces, 1 block, 13 spaces, 1 block, 1 space, 2 blocks, 1 space, 1 block, 14 spaces, 4 blocks, 8 spaces, 1 block, 3 spaces, turn.

Row 17: 3 spaces, 1 block, 8 spaces, 3 blocks, 9 spaces, 6 blocks, 2 spaces, 2 blocks, 2 spaces, 6 blocks, 7 spaces, 1 block, 4 spaces, 3 blocks, 4 spaces, 1 block, 7 spaces, 6 blocks, 2 spaces, 2 blocks, 2 spaces, 6 blocks, 9 spaces, 3 blocks, 8 spaces, 1 block, 3 spaces, turn.

Row 18: 2 spaces, 3 blocks, 7 spaces, 1 block, 9 spaces, 10 blocks, 2 spaces, 10 blocks, 5 spaces, 1 block, 2 spaces, 2 blocks, 1 space, 1 block, 1 space, 2 blocks, 2 spaces, 1 block, 5 spaces, 10 blocks, 2 spaces, 10 blocks, 9 spaces, 1 block, 7 spaces, 3 blocks, 2 spaces, turn.

Row 19: 2 spaces, 3 blocks, 7 spaces, (1 block, 4 spaces) twice, 10 blocks, 2 spaces, 10 blocks, 6 spaces, 2 blocks, 2 spaces, 3 blocks, 2 spaces, 2 blocks, 6 spaces, 10 blocks, 2 spaces, 10 blocks, (4 spaces, 1 block) twice, 7 spaces, 3 blocks, 2 spaces, turn.

Row 20: 2 spaces, 3 blocks, 7 spaces, 1 block, 3 spaces, 2 blocks, 6 spaces, 6 blocks, 2 spaces, 2 blocks, 2 spaces, 6 blocks, 11 spaces, 1 block, 3 spaces, 1 block, 11 spaces, 6 blocks, 2 spaces, 2 blocks, 2 spaces, 6 blocks, 6 spaces, 2 blocks, 3 spaces, 1 block, 7 spaces, 3 blocks, 2 spaces, turn.

Row 21: 2 spaces, 3 blocks, 7 spaces, 1 block, 2 spaces, 3 blocks, 12 spaces, 1 block, 1 space, 2 blocks, 1 space, 1 block, 16 spaces, 1 block, 5 spaces, 1 block, 16 spaces, 1 block, 1 space, 2 blocks, 1 space, 1 block, 12 spaces, 3 blocks, 2 spaces, 1 block, 7 spaces, 3 blocks, 2 spaces, turn.

Row 22: 3 spaces, 1 block, 8 spaces, 1 block, 2 spaces, 4 blocks, 8 spaces, 3 blocks, 1 space, 4 blocks, 1 space, 3 blocks, 12 spaces, 2 blocks, 5 spaces, 2 blocks, 12 spaces, 3 blocks, 1 space, 4 blocks, 1 space, 3 blocks, 8 spaces, 4 blocks, 2 spaces, 1 block, 8 spaces, 1 block, 3 spaces, turn.

Row 23: 3 spaces, 1 block, 8 spaces, 1 block, 2 spaces, 4 blocks, 7 spaces, 4 blocks, (1 space, 4 blocks) twice, 11 spaces, 1 block, 7 spaces, 1 block, 11 spaces, (4 blocks, 1 space) twice, 4 blocks, 7 spaces, 4 blocks, 2 spaces, 1 block, 8 spaces, 1 block, 3 spaces, turn.

Row 24: 2 spaces, 1 block, 1 space, 1 block, 2 spaces, 2 blocks, 3 spaces, 2 blocks, 1 space, 4 blocks, 6 spaces, 4 blocks, 1 space, 1 block, 1 space, 2 blocks, 1 space, 1 block, 1 space, 4 blocks, 10 spaces, 1 block, 4 spaces, 1 block, 2 spaces, 1 block, 10 spaces, 4 blocks, 1 space, 1 block, 1 space, 2 blocks, 1 space, 1 block, 1 space, 4 blocks, 6 spaces, 4 blocks, 1 space, 2 blocks, 3 spaces, 2 blocks, 2 spaces, 1 block, 1 space, 1 block, 2 spaces, turn.

Row 25: 3 spaces, 1 block, 3 spaces, 2 blocks, 4 spaces, 1 block, 1 space, 4 blocks, 6 spaces, 4 blocks, 1 space, 1 block, 1 space, 2 blocks, 1 space, 1 block, 1 space, 4 blocks, 9 spaces, 2 blocks, 1 space, 2 blocks, 4 spaces, 2 blocks, 9 spaces, 4 blocks, 1 space, 1 block, 1 space, 2 blocks, 1 space, 1 block, 1 space, 4 blocks, 6 spaces, 4 blocks, 1 space, 1 block, 4 spaces, 2 blocks, 3 spaces, 1 block, 3 spaces, turn.

Row 26: 3 spaces, 1 block, 3 spaces, 3 blocks, 3 spaces, 1 block, 1 space, 3 blocks, 7 spaces, 3 blocks, (1 space, 2 blocks) 3 times, 1 space, 3 blocks, 2 spaces, 1 block, 3 spaces, 1 block, 2 spaces, 1 block, 4 spaces, 3 blocks, 2 spaces, 1 block, 9 spaces, 3 blocks, 1 space, (2 blocks, 1 space) 3 times, 3 blocks, 7 spaces, 3 blocks, 1 space, 1 block, 3 spaces, 3 blocks, 3 spaces, 1 block, 3 spaces, turn.

Row 27: 2 spaces, 3 blocks, 2 spaces, 4 blocks, 3 spaces, 1 block, 1 space, 2 blocks, 11 spaces, 2 blocks, (1 space, 2 blocks) twice, 10 spaces, (1 block, 2 spaces) twice, 3 blocks, 4 spaces, 1 block, 2 spaces, 2 blocks, 1 space, 3 blocks, 5 spaces, (2 blocks, 1 space) twice, 2 blocks, 11 spaces, 2 blocks, 1 space, 1 block, 3 spaces, 4 blocks, 2 spaces, 3 blocks, 2 spaces, turn.

Row 28: 2 spaces, 3 blocks, 2 spaces, 4 blocks, 3 spaces, 1 block, 1 space, 1 block, 11 spaces, 3 blocks, 1 space, 2 blocks, 1 space, 3 blocks, 4 spaces, (3 blocks, 1 space) twice, 1 block, 3 spaces, 4 blocks, 2 spaces, 1 block, (1 space, 2 blocks) twice, 6 spaces, 3 blocks, 1 space,

2 blocks, 1 space, 3 blocks, 11 spaces, 1 block, 1 space, 1 block, 3 spaces, 4 blocks, 2 spaces, 3 blocks, 2 spaces, turn.

Row 29: 2 spaces, 3 blocks, 3 spaces, 4 blocks, 2 spaces, 1 block, 1 space, 1 block, 11 spaces, 3 blocks, 1 space, 2 blocks, 1 space, 3 blocks, 5 spaces, (1 block, 1 space) twice, 2 blocks, 1 space, 1 block, 2 spaces, 4 blocks, 3 spaces, 1 block, 1 space, 3 blocks, 1 space, 4 blocks, 3 spaces, 3 blocks, 1 space, 2 blocks, 1 space, 3 blocks, 11 spaces, 1 block, 1 space, 1 block, 2 spaces, 4 blocks, 3 spaces, 3 blocks, 2 spaces, turn.

Row 30: 2 spaces, 3 blocks, 5 spaces, 2 blocks, 3 spaces, 1 block, 12 spaces, 2 blocks, (2 spaces, 2 blocks) twice, 7 spaces, 1 block, 3 spaces, 2 blocks, 3 spaces, 3 blocks, 3 spaces, 1 block, 1 space, 3 blocks, 1 space, 2 blocks, 5 spaces, (2 blocks, 2 spaces) twice, 2 blocks, 12 spaces, 1 block, 3 spaces, 2 blocks, 5 spaces, 3 blocks, 2 spaces, turn.

Row 31: 3 spaces, 1 block, 8 spaces, 1 block, 2 spaces, 1 block, 1 space, (4 blocks, 10 spaces) twice, 4 blocks, 1 space, 1 block, 4 spaces, 1 block, 1 space, 1 block, 3 spaces, 1 block, 1 space, 2 blocks, 1 space, 4 blocks, 6 spaces, 4 blocks, 10 spaces, 4 blocks, 1 space, 1 block, 2 spaces, 1 block, 8 spaces, 1 block, 3 spaces, turn.

Row 32: 3 spaces, 1 block, 9 spaces, 1 block, 2 spaces, 5 blocks, 9 spaces, 6 blocks, 6 spaces, 3 blocks, 1 space, 4 blocks, 2 spaces, 3 blocks, (2 spaces, 1 block) twice, 1 space, 7 blocks, 6 spaces, 6 blocks, 9 spaces, 5 blocks, 2 spaces, 1 block, 9 spaces, 1 block, 3 spaces, turn.

Row 33: 2 spaces, 1 block, 1 space, 1 block, 7 spaces, 3 blocks, 1 space, 7 blocks, 7 spaces, 6 blocks, 7 spaces, 7 blocks, 2 spaces, 3 blocks, 1 space, (4 blocks, 1 space) twice, 3 blocks, 6 spaces, 6 blocks, 7 spaces, 7 blocks, 1 space, 3 blocks, 7 spaces, 1 block, 1 space, 1 block, 2 spaces, turn.

Row 34: 3 spaces, 1 block, 8 spaces, 11 blocks, 7 spaces, 6 blocks, 7 spaces, (2 blocks, 1 space) twice, 1 block, 1 space, 9 blocks, 1 space, 5 blocks, 9 spaces, 6 blocks, 7 spaces, 11 blocks, 8 spaces, 1 block, 3 spaces, turn.

Row 35: 3 spaces, 1 block, 6 spaces, 13 blocks, 7 spaces, 6 blocks, 11 spaces, (1 block, 1 space) twice, (4 blocks, 1 space) twice, 1 block, 3 spaces, 1 block, 4 spaces, 2 blocks, 3 spaces, 6 blocks, 7 spaces, 13 blocks, 6 spaces, 1 block, 3 spaces, turn.

Row 36: 2 spaces, 3 blocks, 5 spaces, 5 blocks, (1 space, 2 blocks) twice, 8 spaces, 8 blocks, 2 spaces, 3 blocks, 3 spaces, 3 blocks, 1 space, 1 block, 3 spaces, (1 block, 1 space) twice, 3 blocks, 1 space, 1 block, 3 spaces, 4 blocks, 5 spaces, 8 blocks, 8 spaces, (2 blocks, 1 space) twice, 5 blocks, 5 spaces, 3 blocks, 2 spaces, turn.

Row 37: 2 spaces, 3 blocks, 6 spaces, 5 blocks, 2 spaces, 5 blocks, 6 spaces, 3 blocks, 2 spaces, 3 blocks, 3 spaces, 4 blocks, 1 space, 4 blocks, 4 spaces, 2 blocks, 1 space, 3 blocks, 3 spaces, 1 block, 2 spaces, 3 blocks, 1 space, 3 blocks, 2 spaces, 3 blocks, 2 spaces, 3 blocks, 6 spaces, 5 blocks, 2 spaces, 5 blocks, 6 spaces, 3 blocks, 2 spaces, turn.

Row 38: 2 spaces, 3 blocks, 8 spaces, 3 blocks, 2 spaces, 5 blocks, 7 spaces, 1 block, 1 space, 2 blocks, 1 space, 1 block, 4 spaces, 3 blocks, 4 spaces, 1 block, 2 spaces, 10 blocks, 1 space, 1 block, 5 spaces, 5 blocks, 3 spaces, 1 block, 1 space, 2 blocks, 1 space, 1 block, 7 spaces, 5 blocks, 2 spaces, 3 blocks, 8 spaces, 3 blocks, 2 spaces, turn.

Row 39: 2 spaces, 3 blocks, 6 spaces, 4 blocks, 1 space, 2 blocks, 1 space, 3 blocks, 9 spaces, 4 blocks, 4 spaces, 4 blocks, 3 spaces, 4 blocks, 1 space, 10 blocks, 1 space, 3 blocks, 2 spaces, 6 blocks, 3 spaces, 4 blocks, 9 spaces, 3 blocks, 1 space, 2 blocks, 1 space, 4 blocks, 6 spaces, 3 blocks, 2 spaces, turn.

Row 40: 3 spaces, 1 block, 7 spaces, 11 blocks, 8 spaces, 6 blocks, 2 spaces, 2 blocks, 1 space, 3 blocks, (1 space, 5 blocks, 1 space, 4 blocks) twice, 3 spaces, 2 blocks, 4 spaces, 6 blocks, 8 spaces, 11 blocks, 7 spaces, 1 block, 3 spaces, turn.

Row 41: 3 spaces, 1 block, 6 spaces, 5 blocks, 1 space, 4 blocks, 9 spaces, 8 blocks, 9 spaces, 4 blocks, 2 spaces, 3 blocks, 5 spaces, 5 blocks, 3 spaces, 2 blocks, 4 spaces, 8 blocks, 9 spaces, 4 blocks, 1 space, 5 blocks, 6 spaces, 1 block, 3 spaces, turn.

Row 42: 2 spaces, 1 block, 1 space, 1 block, 6 spaces, 4 blocks, 2 spaces, 3 blocks, 7 spaces, 5 blocks, 2 spaces, 5 blocks, 5 spaces, 2 blocks, 2 spaces, 7 blocks, 4 spaces, 4 blocks, 2 spaces, 3 blocks, 4 spaces, 5 blocks, 2 spaces, 5 blocks, 7 spaces, 3 blocks, 2 spaces, 4 blocks, 6 spaces, 1 block, 1 space, 1 block, 2 spaces, turn.

Row 43: 3 spaces, 1 block, 11 spaces, 1 block, 10 spaces, 3 blocks, 3 spaces, 2 blocks, 3 spaces, 3 blocks, 2 spaces, 2 blocks, 3 spaces, 1 block, 2 spaces, 4 blocks, 2 spaces, 5 blocks, 2 spaces, 1 block, 3 spaces, 2 blocks, 2 spaces, 3 blocks, 3 spaces, 2 blocks, 3 spaces, 3 blocks, 10 spaces, 1 block, 11 spaces, 1 block, 3 spaces, turn.

Side Scallop

Row 44: 3 spaces, 1 block, 11 spaces, 1 block, 6 spaces, 1 block, 3 spaces, 2 blocks, 1 space, turn. 29 squares. This begins side point of scallop.

Row 45: 1 space, 2 blocks, 3 spaces, 2 blocks, 5 spaces, 1 block, 10 spaces, 3 blocks, 2 spaces, turn.

Row 46: 2 spaces, 3 blocks, 4 spaces, 1 block, 3 spaces, 3 blocks, 3 spaces, 4 blocks, 4 spaces, 1 block, 1 space, turn.

Row 47: 1 space, 2 blocks, 4 spaces, 4 blocks, (4 spaces, 1 block) twice, 3 spaces, 3 blocks, 2 spaces, turn.

Row 48: 2 spaces, 3 blocks, 3 spaces, 1 block, 4 spaces, 1 block, 2 spaces, 6 blocks, 4 spaces, 2 blocks, 1 space, turn.

Row 49: 1 space, 3 blocks, 4 spaces, 6 blocks, 1 space, 1 block, 3 spaces, 1 block, 5 spaces, 1 block, 3 spaces, turn.

Row 50: 3 spaces, 1 block, 5 spaces, 1 block, 2 spaces, 8 blocks, 5 spaces, 2 blocks, 1 space, turn. 28 squares.

Row 51: 1 space, 3 blocks, 6 spaces, 3 blocks, 2 spaces, 1 block, 1 space, 2 blocks, 4 spaces, 1 block, 1 space, 1 block, 2 spaces, turn.

Row 52: 3 spaces, 1 block, 6 spaces, 1 block, 1 space, 1 block, 10 spaces, 3 blocks, sk 2 st, dtr in next st, turn. 27 squares.

Row 53: 3 spaces, 1 block, 9 spaces, 3 blocks, 6 spaces, 1 block, 3 spaces, turn. 26 squares.

Row 54: 2 spaces, 3 blocks, 5 spaces, 2 blocks, 4 spaces, 2 blocks, 3 spaces, 1 block, sk 2 st, dtr in next st, turn. 23 squares.

Row 55: 1 space, 1 block, 3 spaces, 3 blocks, 2 spaces, 1 block, 6 spaces, 3 blocks, 2 spaces, turn. 22 squares.

Row 56: 2 spaces, 3 blocks, 6 spaces, 1 block, 1 space, 4 blocks, 2 spaces, 2 blocks, 1 space, turn.

Row 57: 1 space, 2 blocks, 3 spaces, 6 blocks, 5 spaces, 3 blocks, 2 spaces, turn.

Row 58: 3 spaces, 1 block, 6 spaces, 1 block, 2 spaces, 2 blocks, 4 spaces, 2 blocks, 1 space, turn.

Row 59: 1 space, 3 blocks, 7 spaces, 2 blocks, 5 spaces, 1 block, 3 spaces, turn.

Row 60: 2 spaces, 1 block, 1 space, 1 block, 4 spaces, 1 block, 7 spaces, 3 blocks, sk 2 st, dtr in next st, turn. 21 squares.

Row 61: 1 space, 3 blocks, 6 spaces, 1 block, 5 spaces, 1 block, 3 spaces, turn. 20 squares.

Row 62: Sl st over 2 spaces, 1 space, 5 blocks, 5 spaces, 6 blocks, sk 2 st, dtr in next st, turn.

Row 63: 2 spaces, 13 blocks, sk 2 st, dtr in next st, turn. 16 squares.

Row 64: 2 spaces, 9 blocks, 2 spaces, turn. 13 squares.

Row 65: Sl st over 2 spaces, 3 spaces, 3 blocks, 3 spaces, turn. 9 squares.

Row 66: Sl st over 3 spaces, 3 spaces; fasten off neatly. 3 squares.

Tiny Scallop

Skip 1 space beyond end of 44th row, and fasten in top of next dc, and make the tiny point or scallop thus:

Row 67: 1 space, 4 blocks, 1 space, turn. 6 squares.

Row 68: 1 space, 4 blocks, sk 2 st, dtr in next st, turn.

Row 69: 1 space, 2 blocks, sk 2 st, dtr in next st, turn. 4 squares.

Row 70: 2 spaces; fasten off. 2 squares.

Fasten in at beginning of Row 43 on other side, and work from Row 44 to Row 70.

Center Scallop

Skip 1 space beyond a tiny point, fasten in next dc, and proceed with the center point:

Row 1: 1 space, 2 blocks, 2 spaces, 1 block, 3 spaces, 2 blocks, 3 spaces, 4 blocks, 1 space, 4 blocks, 3 spaces, 3 blocks, 2 spaces, 1 block, 2 spaces, 2 blocks, 1 space, turn. 37 squares.

Row 2: 1 space, 2 blocks, 2 spaces, 1 block, 1 space, 3 blocks, 4 spaces, 9 blocks, 4 spaces, 2 blocks, 2 spaces, 1 block, 2 spaces, 2 blocks, 1 space, turn.

Row 3: 1 space, 1 block, 4 spaces, 1 block, 1 space, 3 blocks, 4 spaces, 7 blocks, 4 spaces, 4 blocks, 5 spaces, 1 block, 1 space, turn.

Row 4: 1 space, 2 blocks, 4 spaces, 2 blocks, 1 space, 1 block, 4 spaces, (1 block 1 space) 3 times, 1 block, 4 spaces, 1 block, 1 space, 1 block, 5 spaces, 2 blocks, 1 space, turn.

Row 5: 1 space, 2 blocks, 5 spaces, 1 block, 1 space, 2 blocks, 4 spaces, (1 block, 1 space) twice, 1 block, 4 spaces, 4 spaces, 2 blocks, 1 space, 1 block, 5 spaces, 2 blocks, 1 space, turn.

Row 6: 1 space, 3 blocks, 4 spaces, 4 blocks, 4 spaces, 2 blocks, 1 space, 2 blocks, 4 spaces, 4 blocks, 4 spaces, 3 blocks, sk 2 st, dtr in next st, turn.

Row 7: 1 space, 2 blocks, 5 spaces, 3 blocks, 4 spaces, (1 block, 1 space) twice, 1 block, 4 spaces, 3 blocks, 5 spaces, 2 blocks, 1 space, turn. 35 squares.

Row 8: 1 space, 3 blocks, 5 spaces, 2 blocks, 4 spaces, 2 blocks, 1 space, 2 blocks, 4 spaces, 2 blocks, 5 spaces, 3 blocks, sk 2 st, dtr in next st, turn.

Row 9: 1 space, 3 blocks, 4 spaces, 1 block, 5 spaces, (1 block, 1 space) twice, 1 block, 5 spaces, 1 block, 4 spaces, 3 blocks, sk 2 st, dtr in next st, turn. 33 squares.

Row 10: 3 spaces, 1 block, 9 spaces, 2 blocks, 1 space, 2 blocks, 9 spaces, 1 block, 3 spaces, turn. 31 squares.

Row 11: Sl st over 3 spaces, 1 space, 1 block, 8 spaces, 5 blocks, 8 spaces, 1 block, 1 space, sk 2 st, dtr in next st, turn. 25 squares.

Row 12: 1 space, 1 block, 6 spaces, 7 blocks, 6 spaces, 1 block, 1 space, turn. 23 squares.

Row 13: 1 space, 2 blocks, 3 spaces, 11 blocks, 3 spaces, 2 blocks, 1 space, turn.

Row 14: 1 space, 2 blocks, 2 spaces, 13 blocks, 2 spaces, 2 blocks, 1 space, turn.

Row 15: 1 space, 2 blocks, 17 spaces, 2 blocks, 1 space, turn.

Row 16: 1 space, 3 blocks, 15 spaces, 3 blocks, sk 2 st, dtr in next st, turn.

Row 17: 1 space, 3 blocks, 13 spaces, 3 blocks, sk 2 st, dtr in next st, turn. 21 squares.

Row 18: 1 space, 3 blocks, 11 spaces, 3 blocks, 1 space, turn. 19 squares.

Row 19: 1 space, 6 blocks, 5 spaces, 6 blocks, sk 2 st, dtr in next st, turn.

Row 20: 2 spaces, 13 blocks, 2 spaces, turn. 17 squares.

Row 21: Sl st over 2 spaces, 2 spaces, 9 blocks, 2 spaces, turn. 13 squares.

Row 22: Sl st over 2 spaces, 3 spaces, 3 blocks, 3 spaces, turn. 9 squares.

Row 23: Sl st over 3 spaces, 3 spaces; fasten off. 3 squares.

Tropical Flowers Chart

Chain 338.

Odd rows are worked left to right. Even rows are worked right to left.

Begin rows with ch 5 for first space.

Refer to written instructions for decreases and scallops.

Finishing

Edging

Fill each straight space all around the edge with 3 sc; make 7 in corner spaces and 4 in curved spaces.

Tassels

Wind the thread sixty times over a four-inch card, slip off, fold in half, tie tightly about one-fourth inch from the fold for the head of the tassel and clip the ends evenly. Make 5 tassels.

Attach a tassel at the center of each scallop, joining to the scallop with a chain put through the head of the tassel.

Hints & Tips

Use the best thread. Don't try to save a few pennies on the thread. You're not just making lace, you're making an heirloom!

Wash your hands before you pick up your project to work on. Keeping your hands clean while you work will help to avoid stains on your piece of lace.

When you're finished, weave in ends of thread by pulling the thread through several stitches with your hook.

To block your lace, dampen it and use a warm iron to block it in to shape. I like to use a little bit of spray starch to finish it off.

Filet crochet patterns are made up of two elements. The first is the space, which is made up of a double crochet, chain two, skip two stitches, and double crochet in the next stitch. The second is the block, which is made of a double crochet, double crochet in the next two stitches, and double crochet in the next stitch.

You can follow a chart instead of a written pattern (a chart is included with this pattern). When you use the chart, you just need to remember that the beginning of each row starts with either chain three (for a block) or chain five (for a space). You can also use the chart to check your progress if you're using the written instructions.

Filet crochet blocks and times are not quite square, so your finished project won't look as squared off as the chart.

Visit http://claudiabotterweg.com/crochet for tips, hints and more about lace crochet.

I hope you enjoyed making this beautiful piece of lace. Tell your friends where you got the pattern.

About the Editor

Claudia Botterweg learned how to crochet in third grade, and by the time she left home for college she had completed 8 rows on a ripple afghan. At Ohio State, she found herself living across the street from a vintage clothing store, and spent most of her budget on vintage clothes. She began repairing clothes in exchange for store credit. One of her tasks was to make camisoles with vintage crocheted lace yokes.

After college, Claudia inherited a tin full of several used balls of tatting thread, a tatting shuttle, and a size 14 steel crochet hook from her grandmother. She made some lace edgings from an old crochet pattern book, became fascinated with lace, and graduated to making doilies. In the 1980s, she made hundreds of lace collars and sold them at craft fairs. She also designed her own camisole yokes and made camisoles to sell.

Recently, Claudia acquired a stack of vintage patterns. She has been busily translating the patterns from vintage instructions, making them easy for beginning and intermediate crocheters to read. She is writing instructions when only charts were provided, and making charts when only written instructions were provided.

Claudia hopes that a new generation of crocheters will learn how to make beautiful lace to decorate themselves, their friends and families, and their homes.

http://ClaudiaBotterweg.com

More Patterns from Claudia Botterweg

Grape & Leaf Altar Lace
Ivy Lace Scarf End
Beverly Lace & Insertion
Dogwood Blossom Lace Curtain
Two Peacocks Lace Curtain
Quilt Block Lace Edging & Insertion
Two Dragons Lace Curtain
Lyre Lace Scarf End
Butterfly Lace Camisole Yoke
Daffodil Lace Curtain
Rose Lace & Insertion
Daffodil Altar Lace
Garden Trellis Lace Centerpiece
Elegant Dragons Lace Curtain
Regal Peacocks Lace Curtain
Morning Glory Lace & Insertion
Nottingham Apple Lace Luncheon Set Filet Crochet Pattern
Lion Lace Panel Filet Crochet Pattern
Butterfly Lace Table Runner Filet Crochet Pattern
Crochet Journal
Knitting Journal
Quilting Journal
Rose Insertion Filet Crochet Pattern
Diamonds Insertion & Edging Filet Crochet Pattern
Tall Ship Lace Filet Crochet Pattern
Two Spring Lace Panels Filet Crochet Pattern

Printed in Great Britain
by Amazon